Colorado State Capitol

Denver

Jane Moorman

There is a saying, "It was a Friday night and it seemed like a good idea at the time." That sums up the beginning of the State Capitols Project.

When I told my brother of my idea of photographing state capitols, he said, "You do know there are 50 states and two of them you can't drive to."

Each capitol has its own unique beauty that reflects the state's personality when it was built.

Jane Moorman, photographer

The Mile High Capitol

Colorado's capitol is truly a mile high. It was constructed at the elevation of 5,280 feet above sea level. The words "One Mile Above Sea Level" is inscribed into the granite of the 15th step on the west entrance stairs.

Since the construction, studies have determined that the exact mile high location is on the 13th step. In 2003 a new marker was placed there.

The Corinthian architectural style building was designed by Elijah E. Myers of Detroit, who also designed the capitols of Michigan and Texas.

Construction began in 1886. Myers was dismissed from the project in 1889. The building was not completed until 1908 when the dome was leafed gold.

The building was constructed with Colorado materials, except for the brass and oak trimming. Granite was quarried in Gunnison. The interior wainscoting and pillar facings are of Colorado onyx. Foundation and walls are Fort Collins sandstone.

Colorado's Capitol in Denver shines golden from the exterior gold-paneled dome to the brass grand stairway and each floor's banisters.

The state's pride in the diverse people that developed the state is captured in stained-glass windows throughout the building.

The women who helped settle the state are honored with a quilt that shows the various women and how they served their communities.

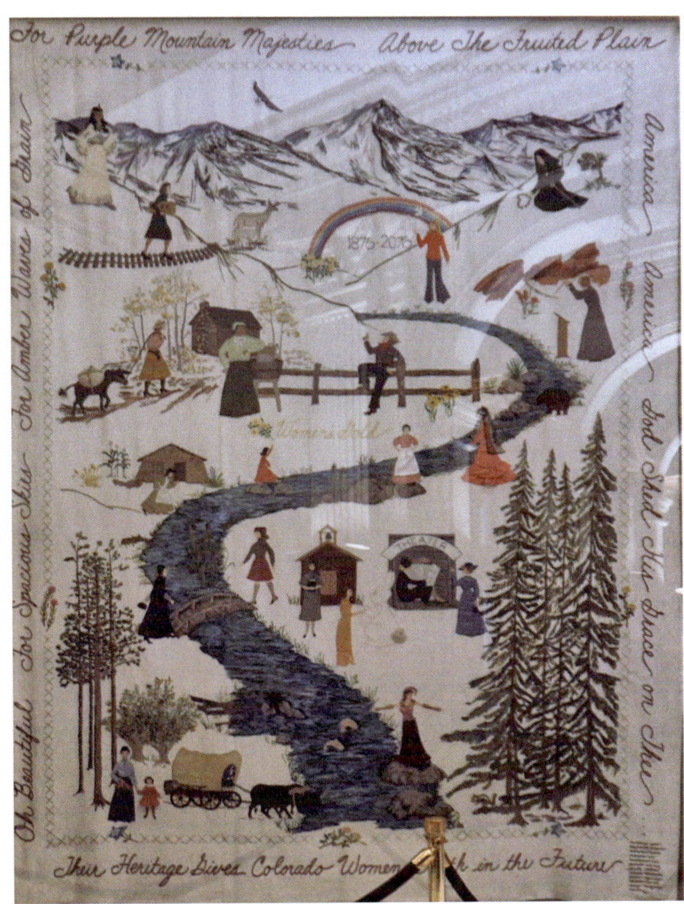

A series of murals around the grand staircase shows the interaction of people with the water as it depicts Thomas Hornsby Ferril poem.

Golden Dome

A gold-leaf dome and glass globe crowns the Colorado white granite building 272 feet above the ground. Gilding of the copper dome was added in 1908 to commemorate the Colorado Gold Rush.

In 2012 restoration of the dome began. The project repaired damage and restored the exterior painted circular tower above the roof of the capitol, and regild the famous gold dome.

Between the inside and outside layers of the dome, a narrow, winding stairway leads to a public observation deck.

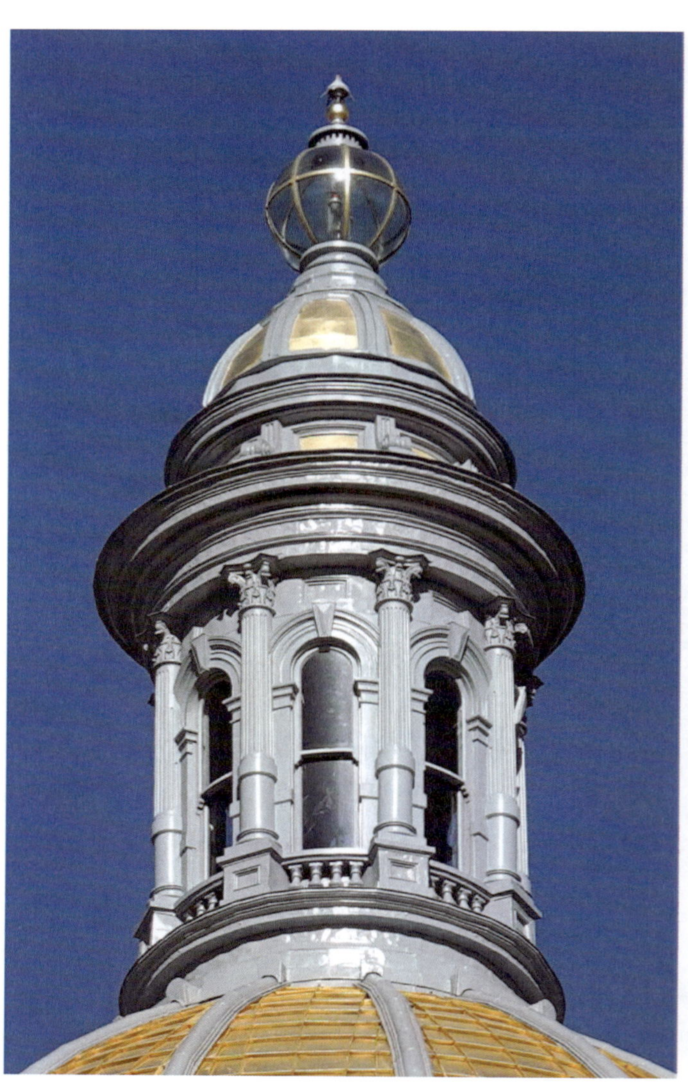

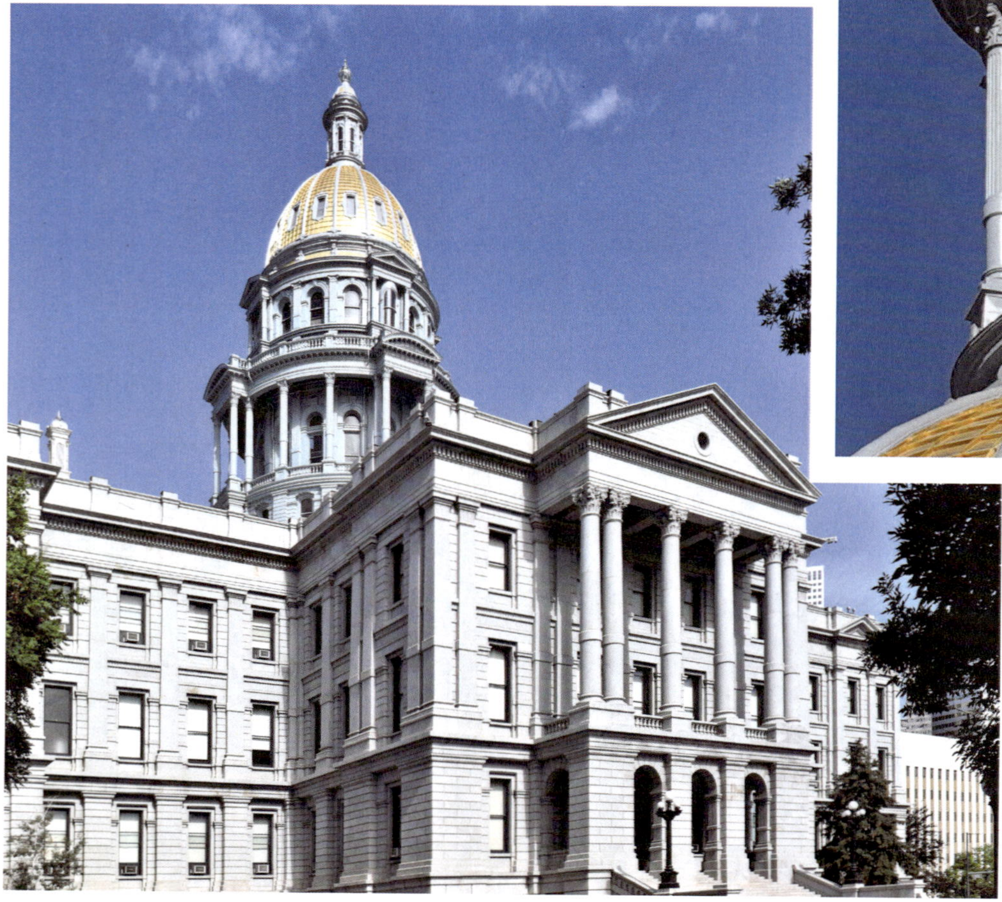

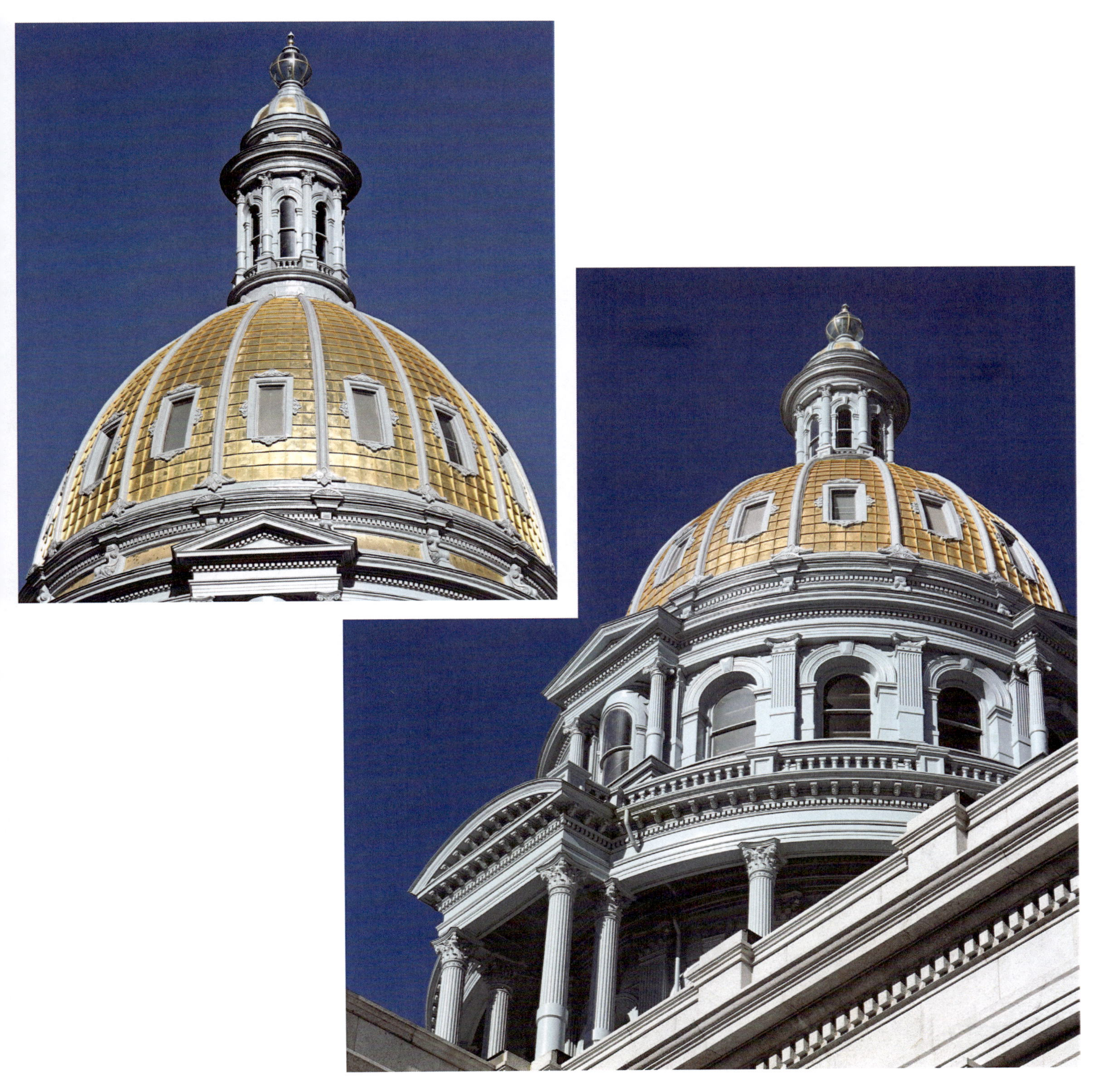

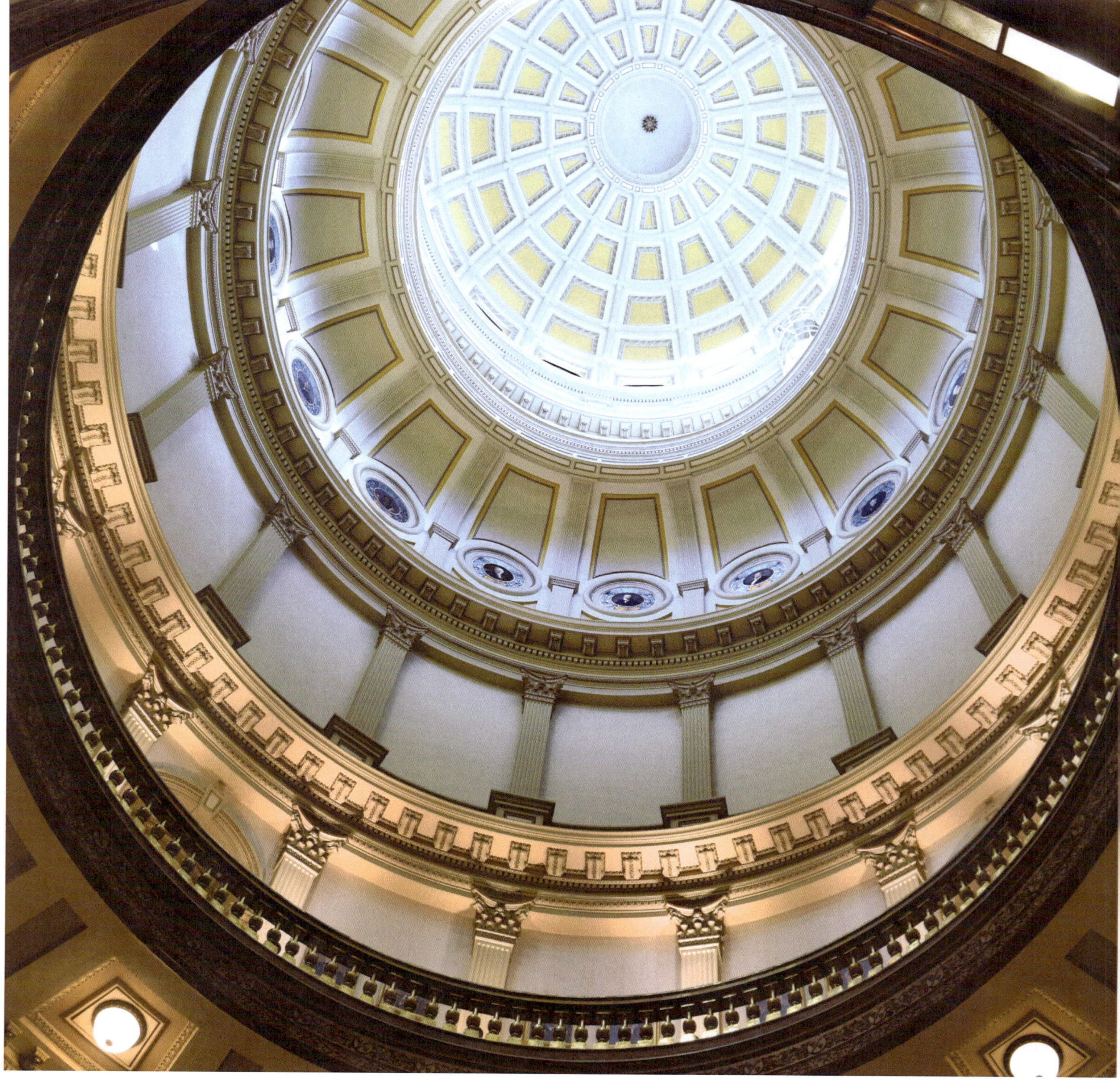

Inside the Rotunda Dome

Visitors may see the upper level of the dome during a guided tour. After climbing stairs to the viewing level, visitors have a magnificent view of Denver on a balcony around the outside of the dome. Inside they may get a closer look at the dome and pilaster capitals, as well as the stained-glass Hall of Fame honoring outstanding Colorado citizens.

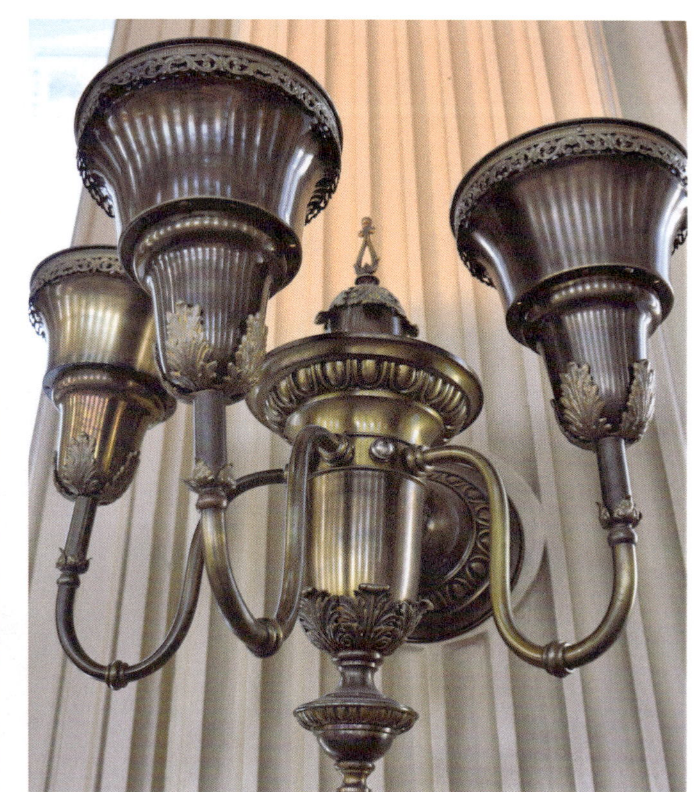

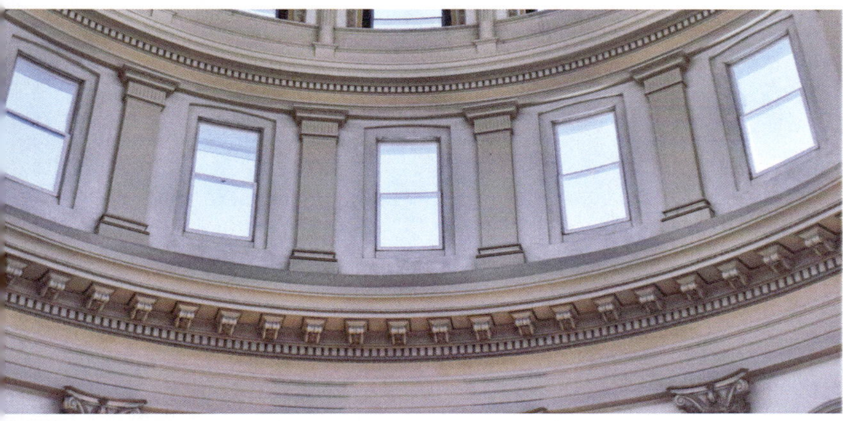

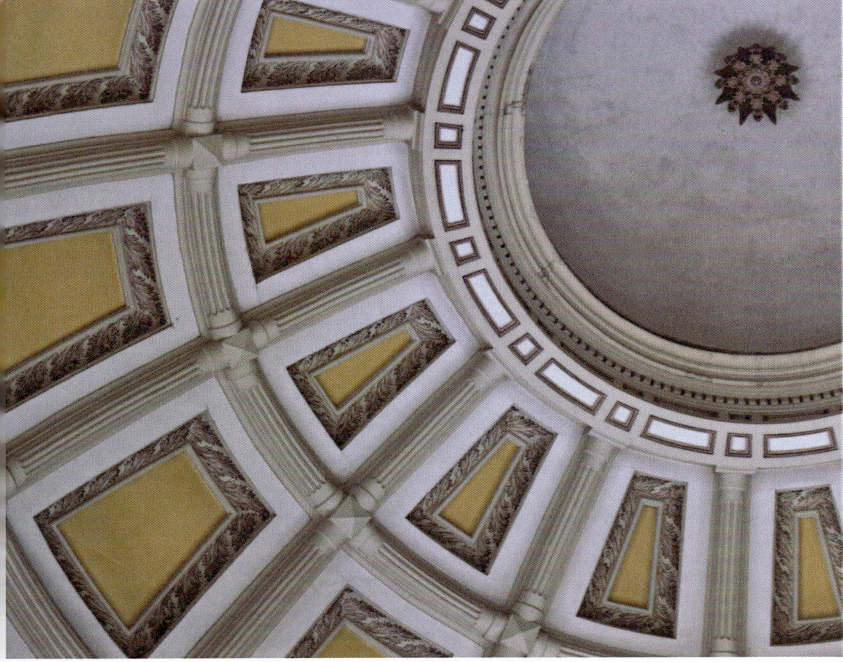

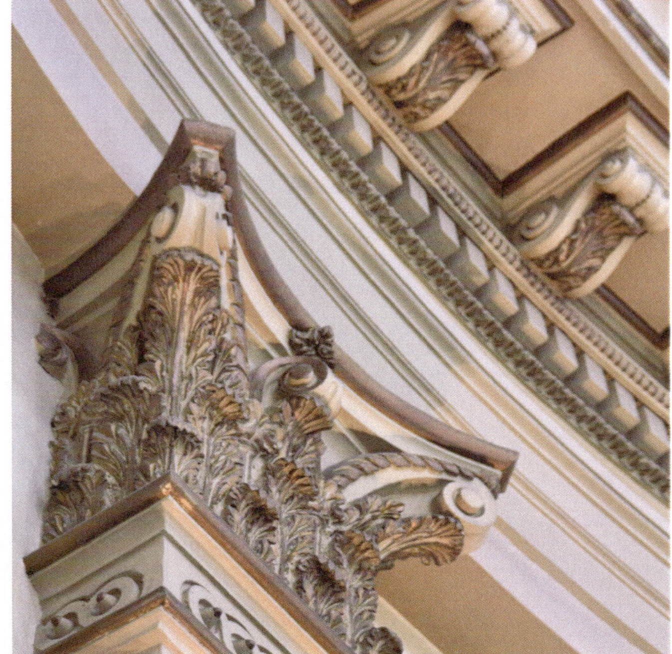

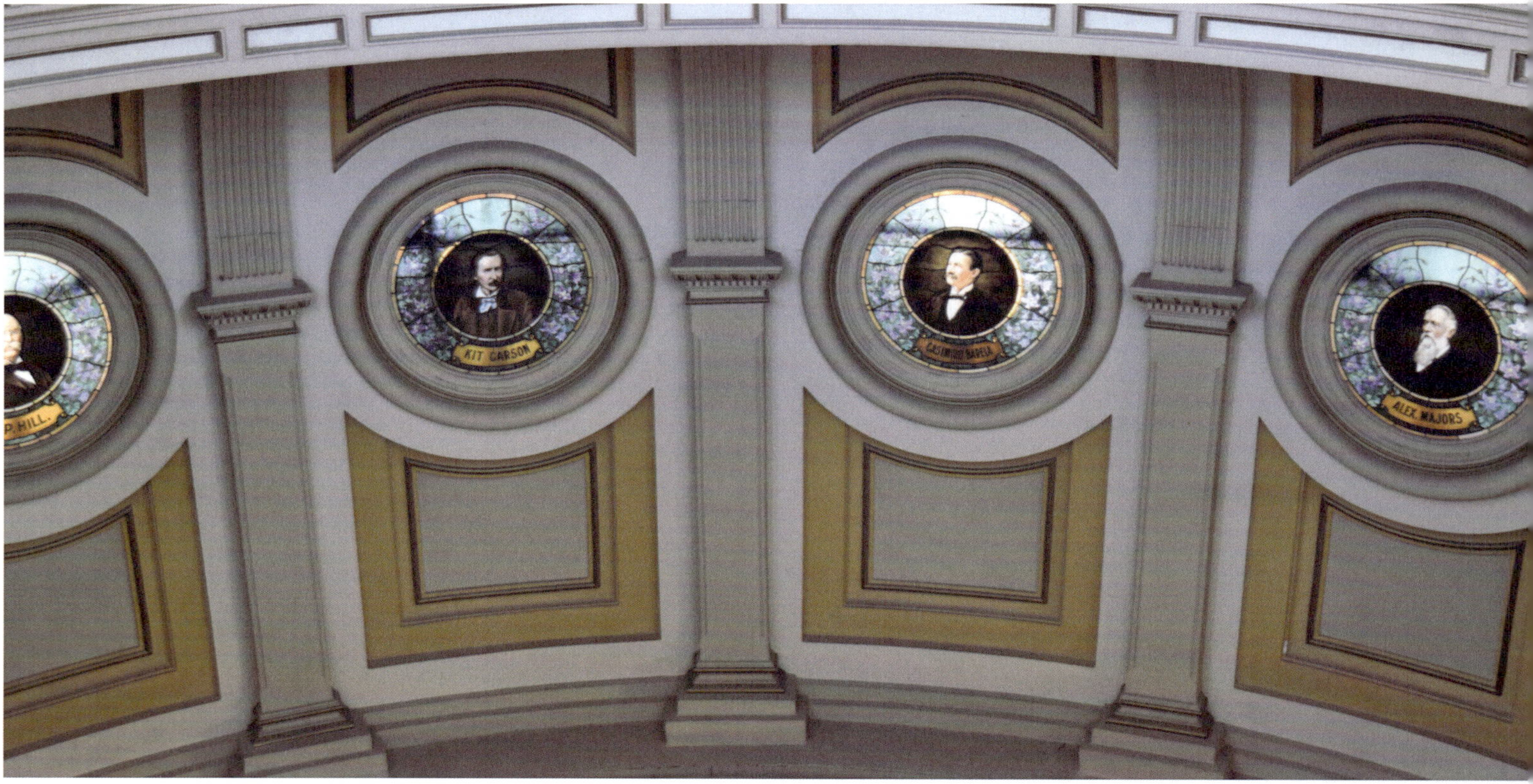

Hall of Fame Stained-Glass

Circling the rotunda dome four-stories above the ground floor is Colorado's Hall of Fame or Circle of Fame as some call it. Fifteen men and one woman are honored with stained-glass created by Martin Faith of Denver Stained Glass. There are descriptions of each of these individuals on the viewing balcony railing.

Frances Jacobs, the solo woman honored, was a prominent figure in local charity organization. She helped establish the state's first free kindergarten, National Jewish Hospital, and was a founder of the United Way.

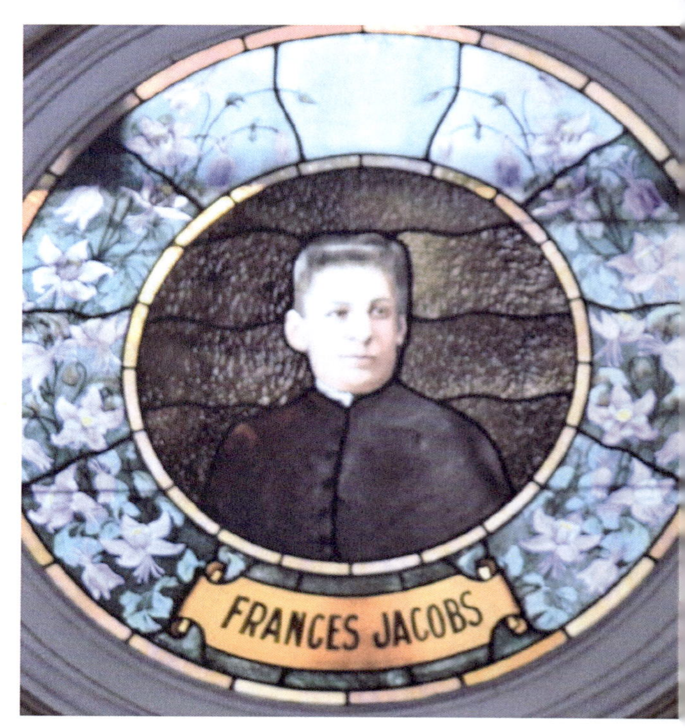

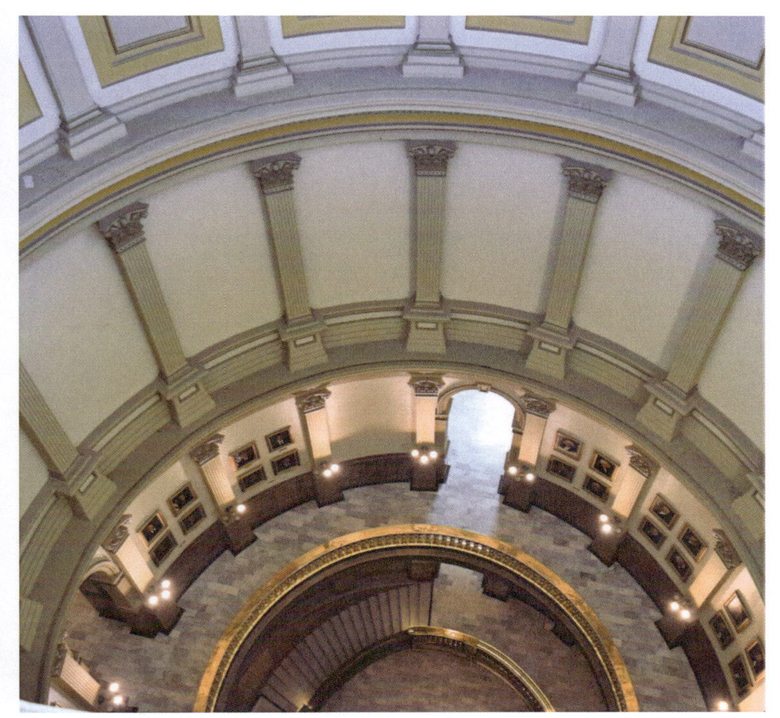

Looking Down

From the observation deck inside the dome, visitors can look down through the five level of the dome to the rotunda first floor.

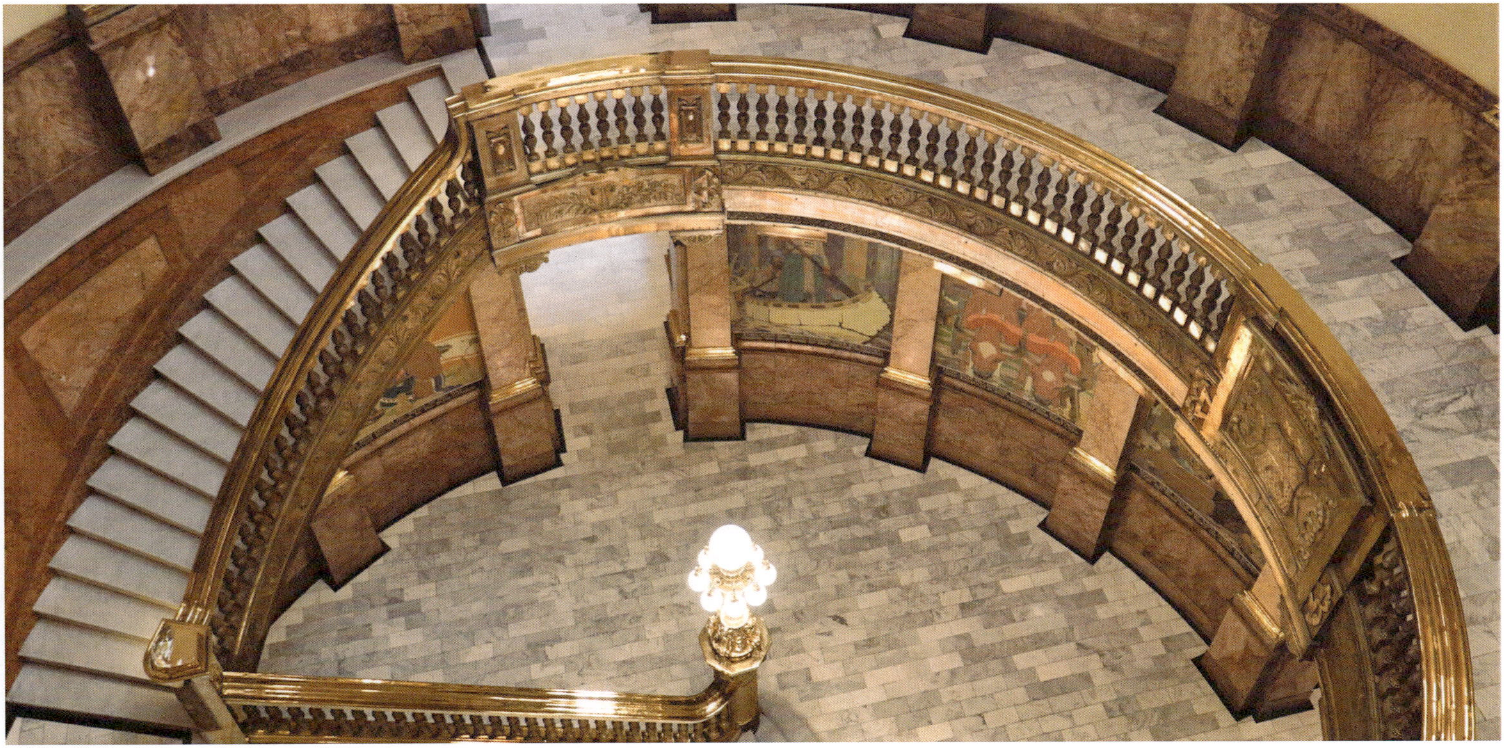

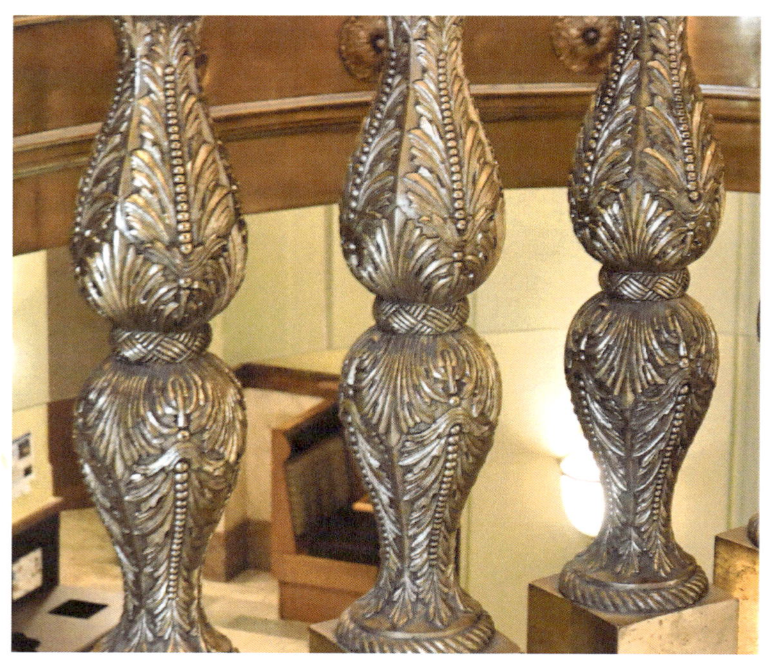
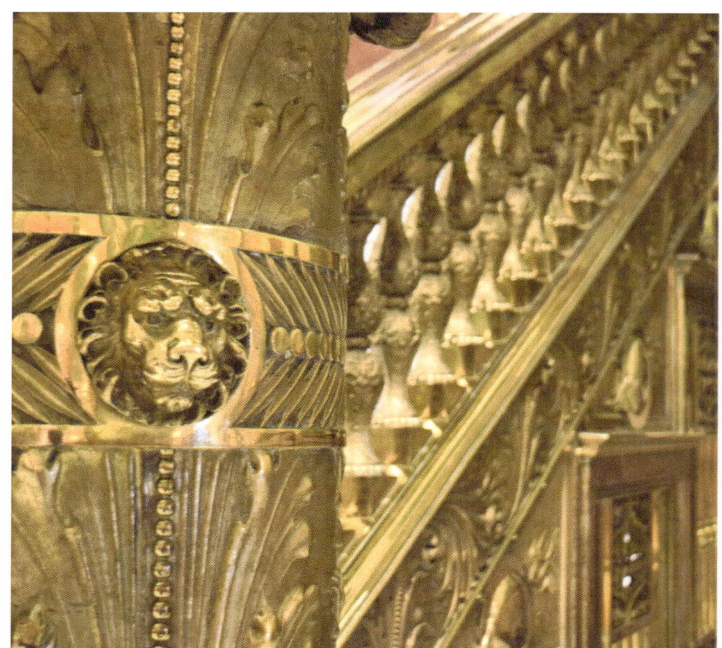

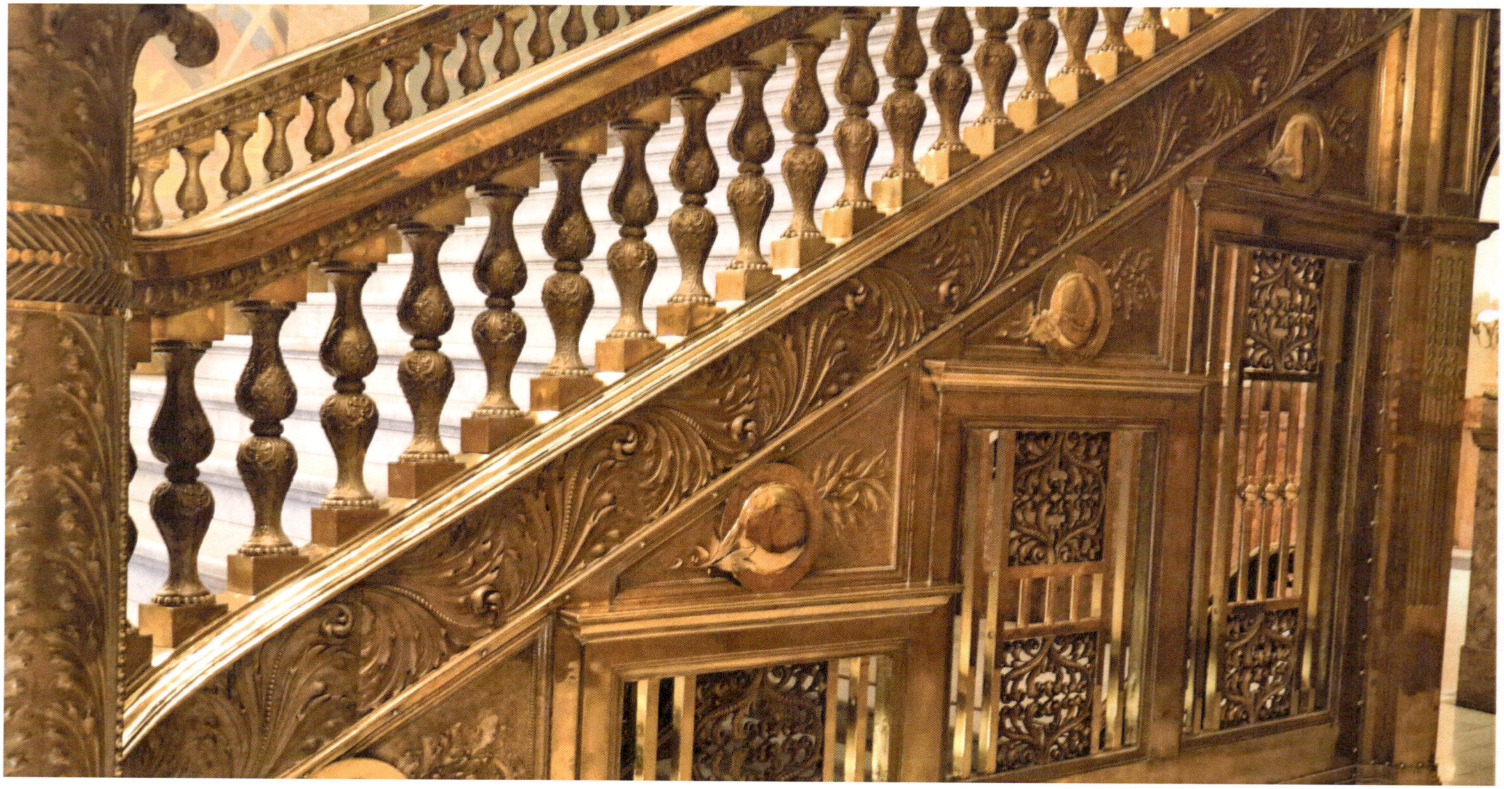

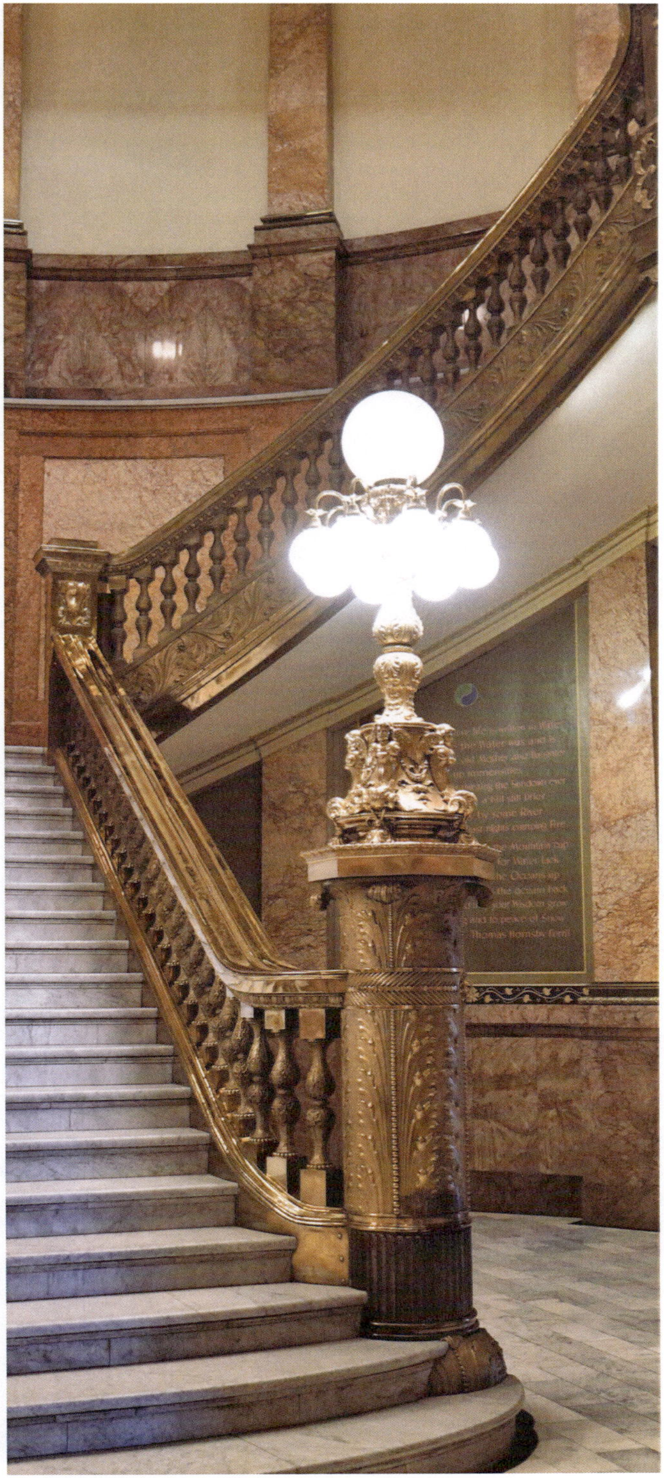

Grand Stairway

The grand staircase rises from the first floor and encircles the second floor of the rotunda.

The brass railing, newels and balustrades shine golden. Angles surround the base of the newel chandelier. A lion protrudes from the starting newel. Detailed etching highlights the balustrades and side panel.

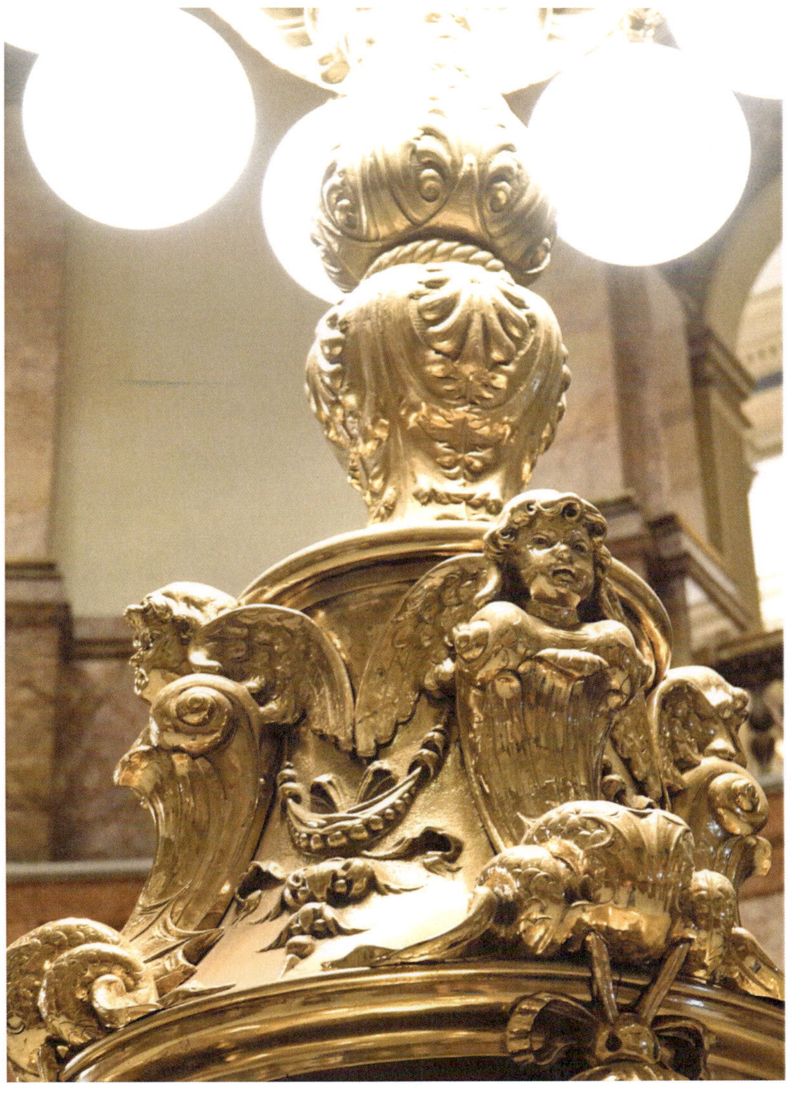

Colorado Onyx

The interior wainscoting and pillar facings are of Colorado onyx, a rare marble from nearby Beulah, CO, which features variations in pink, mauve, and maroon colors.

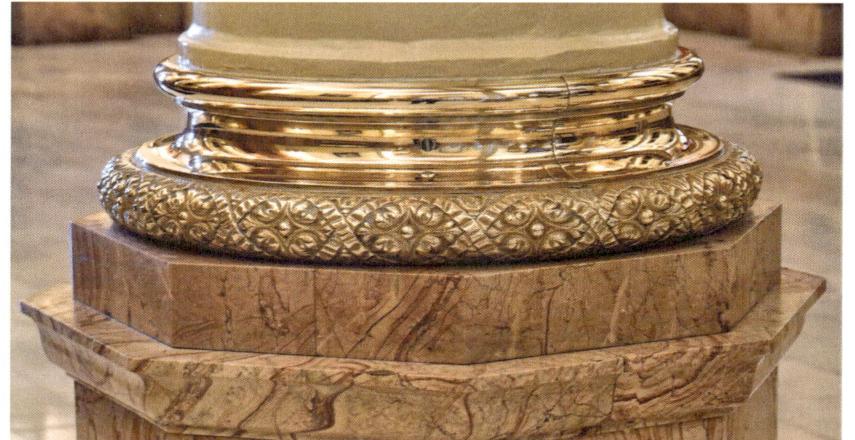

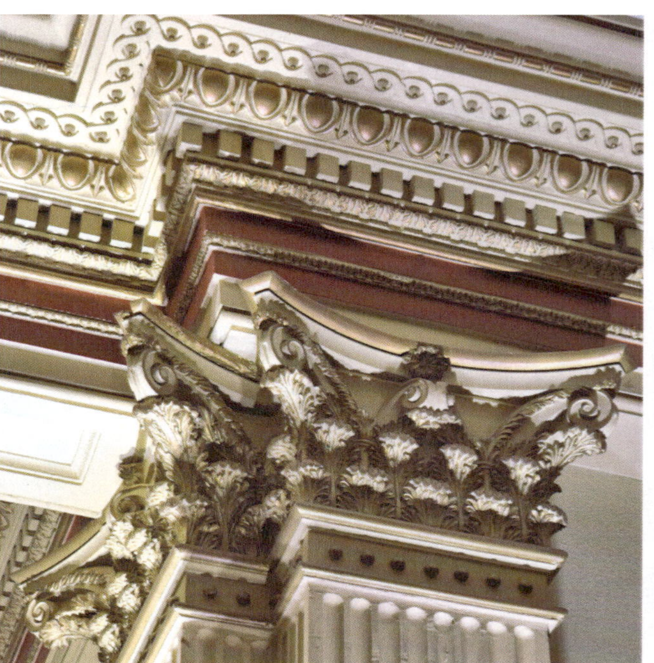

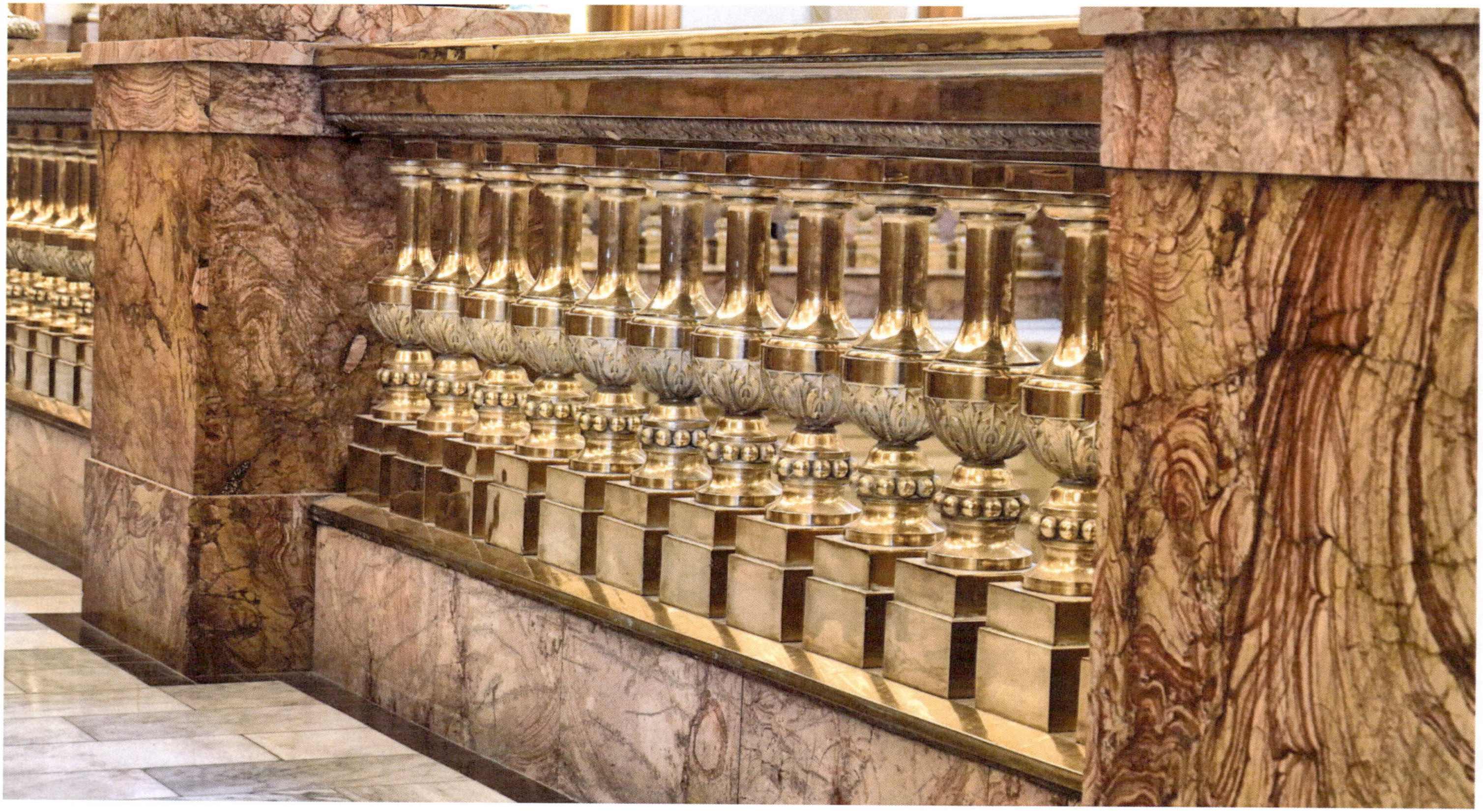

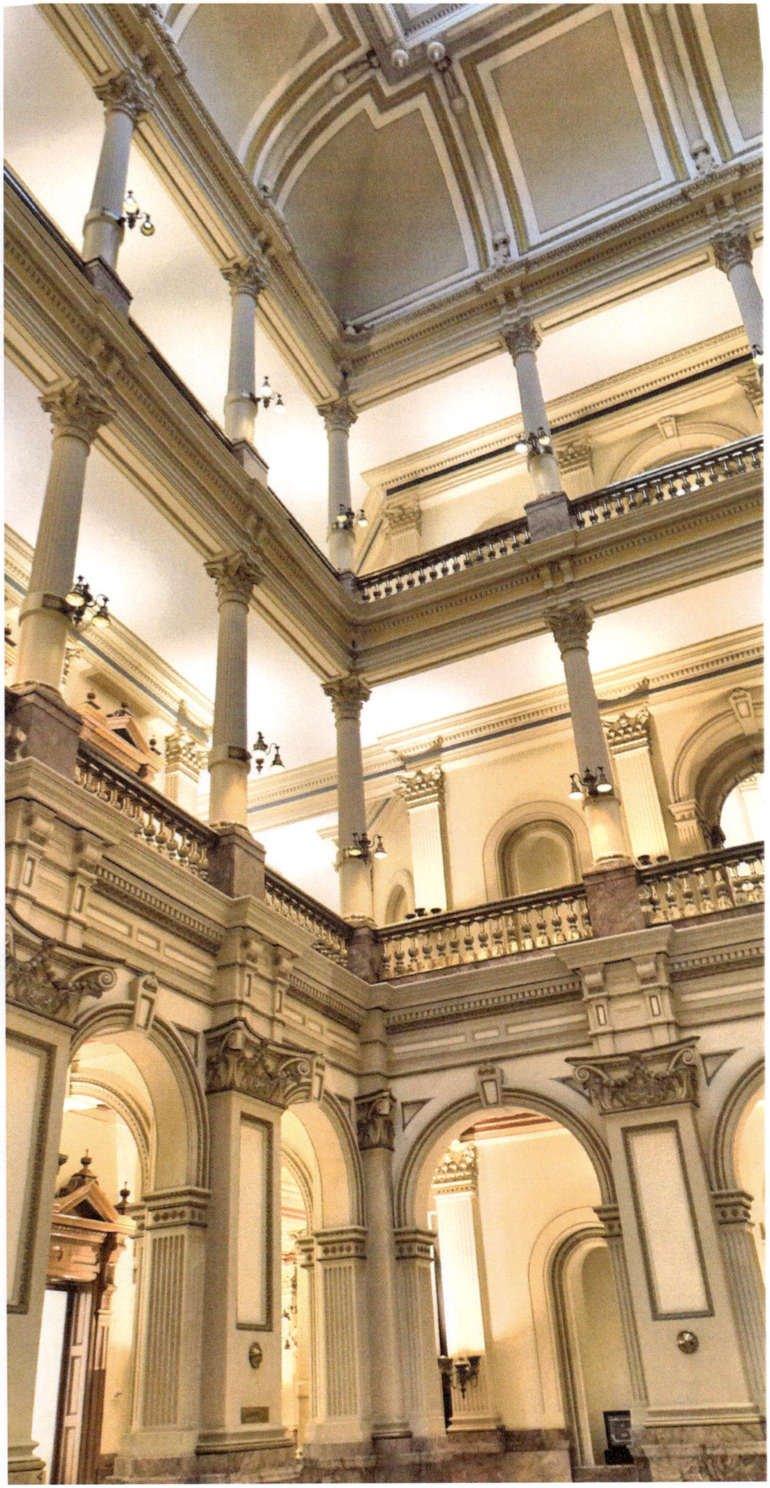

European Flair

Corinthian architectural style gives the three-floor atrium around the rotunda an European flair.

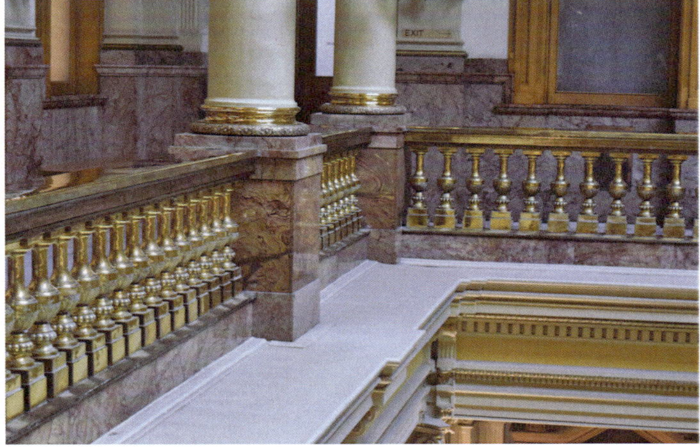

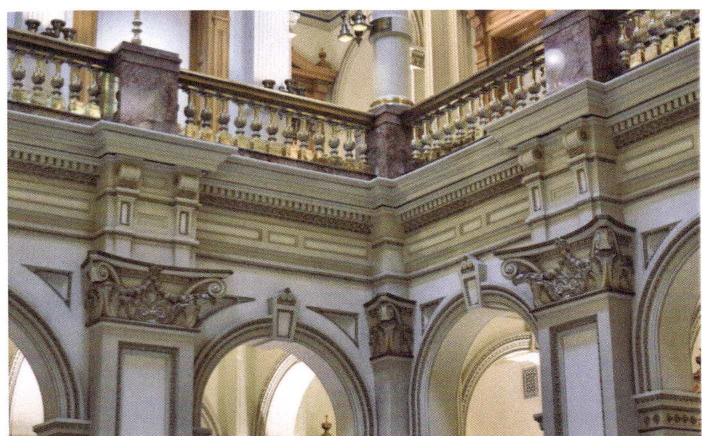

Senate Chamber

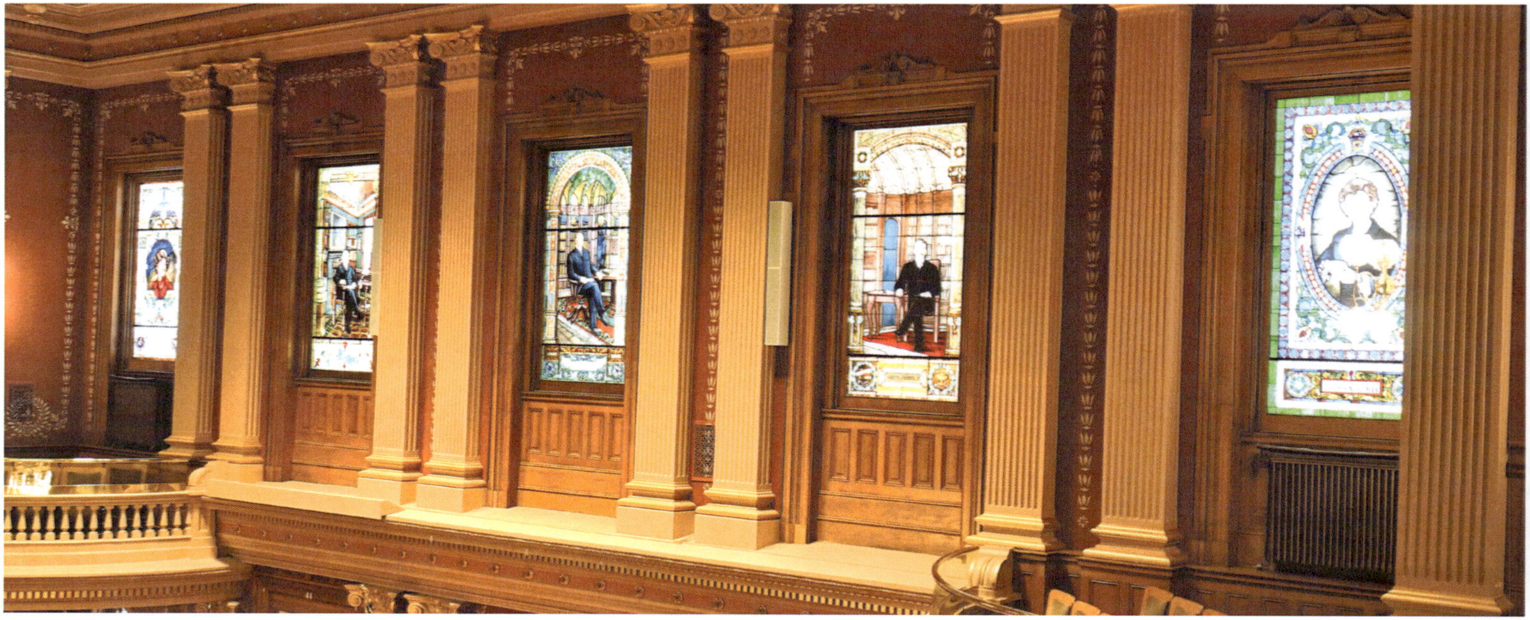

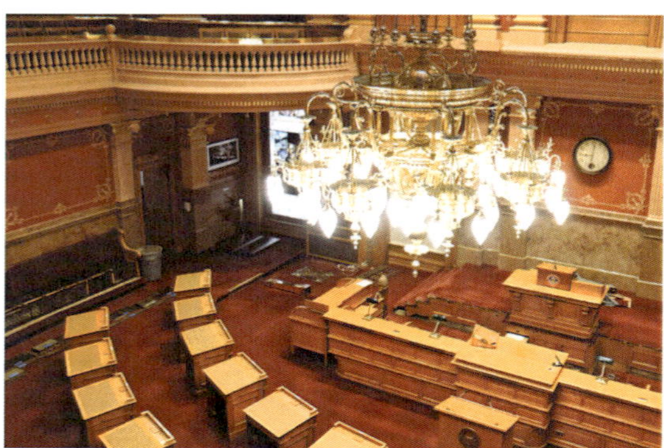

Stained-glass portraits honor influential individuals in Colorado's history. Similar brass chandeliers hang in the Senate, House and Old Supreme Court chambers.

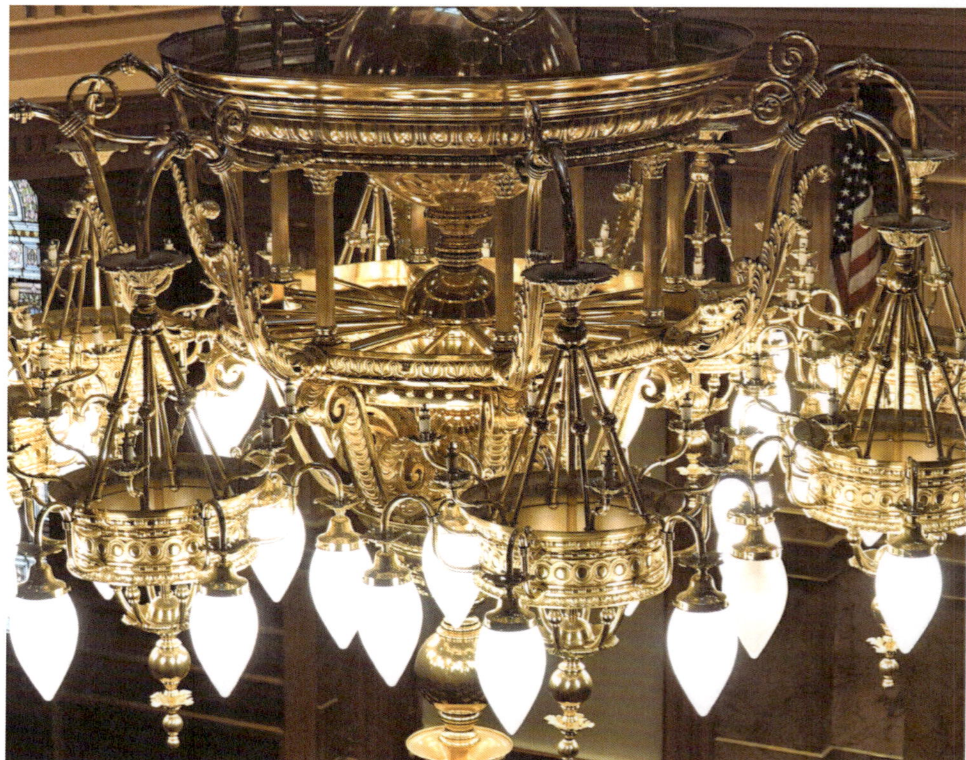

House of Representatives Chamber

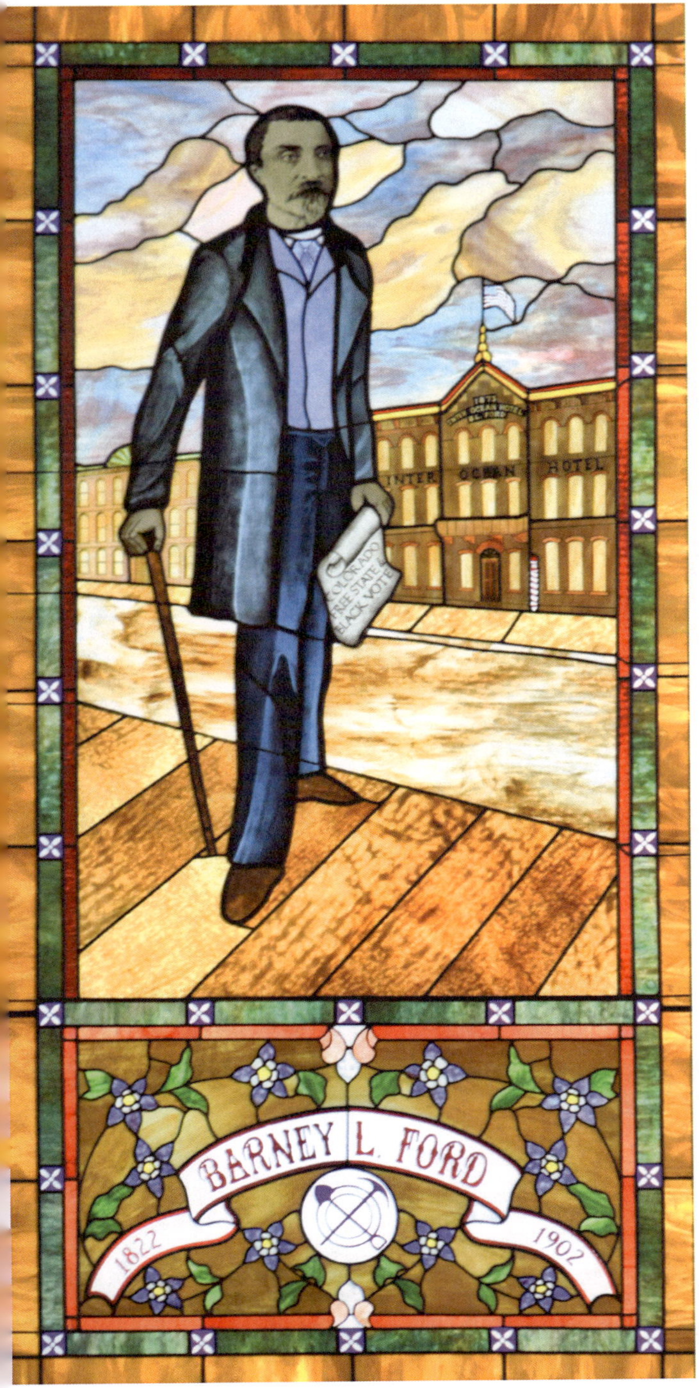

The stencil-painted ceilings have the same pattern in both legislative chambers, with background color re-flecting the chamber's color scheme: green for the House and red for the Senate.

Above the dais in the House chamber is a stained-glass portrait of Barney Ford, an escaped slave who later became a wealthy business man and civil-rights pioneer in Colorado.

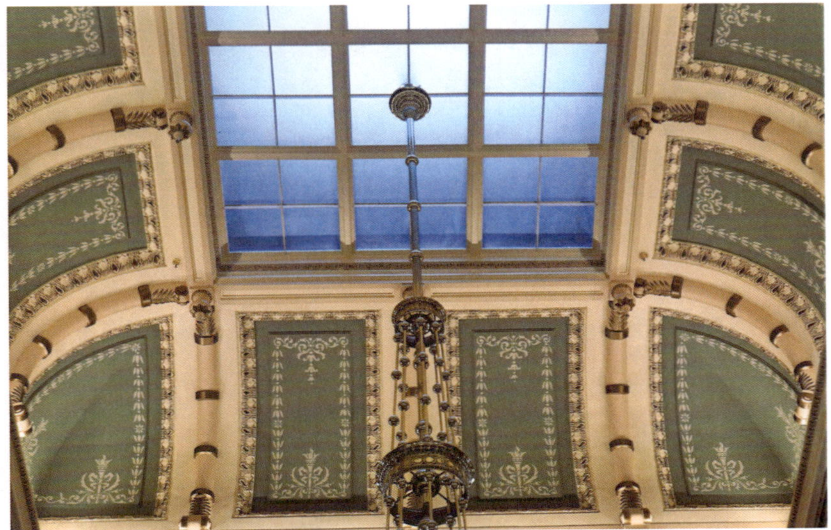

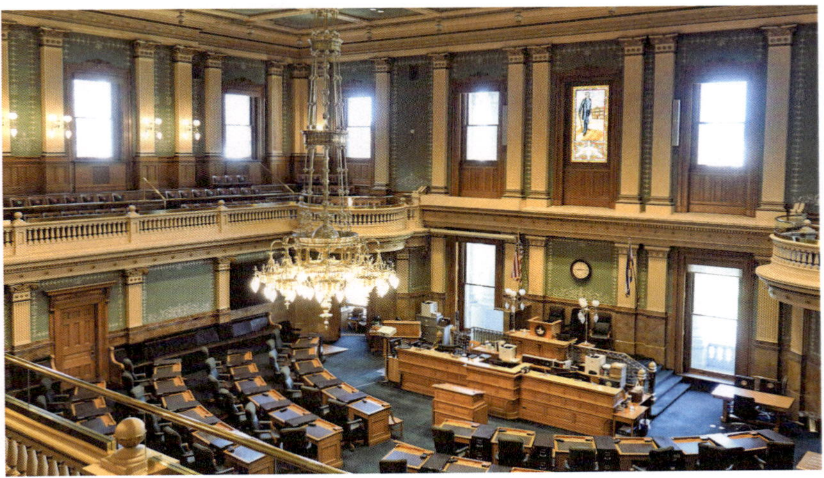

Old Supreme Court Chamber

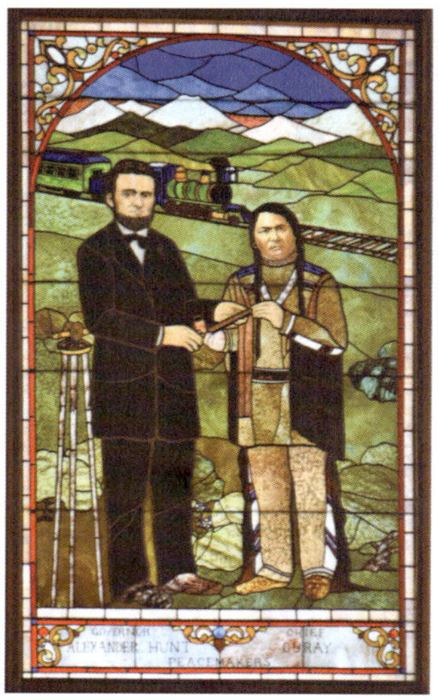 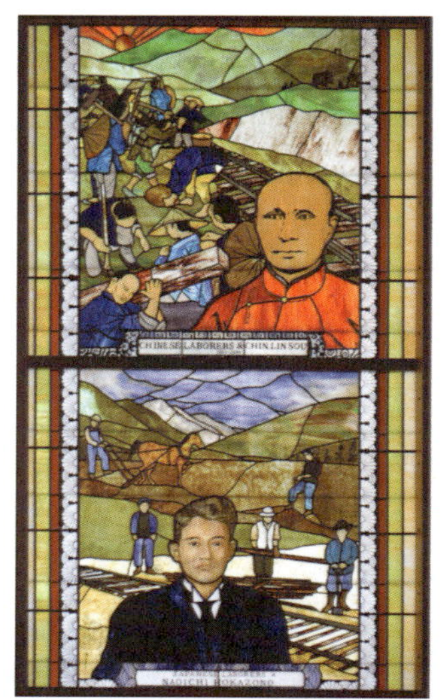 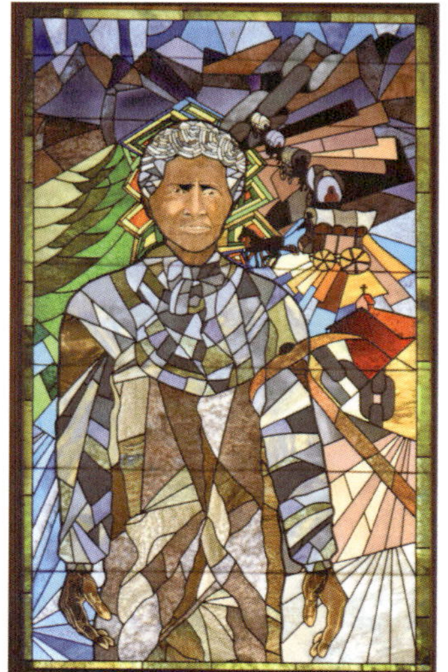 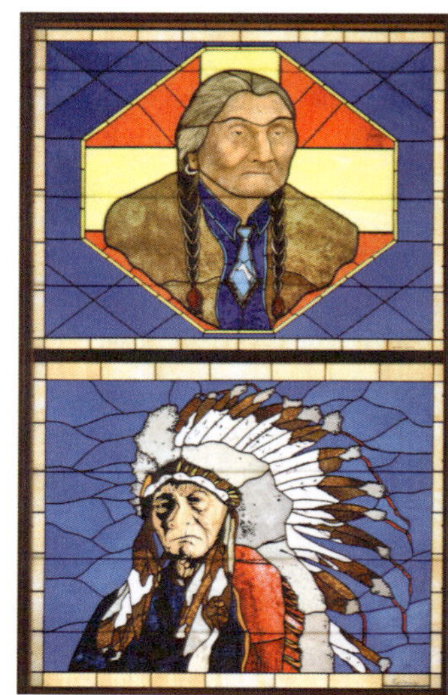

Heritage Windows in the Old Supreme Court chamber honor Latino, Black, Indigenous, and Asian individuals in Colorado history. Among the seven stained-glass portraits installed in 1977. Gov. Alexander Hunt and Chief Ouray are honored as peacemakers. Others included are Chinese community leader Chin Lin Sou and Japanese entrepreneur Naoichi Hokazono

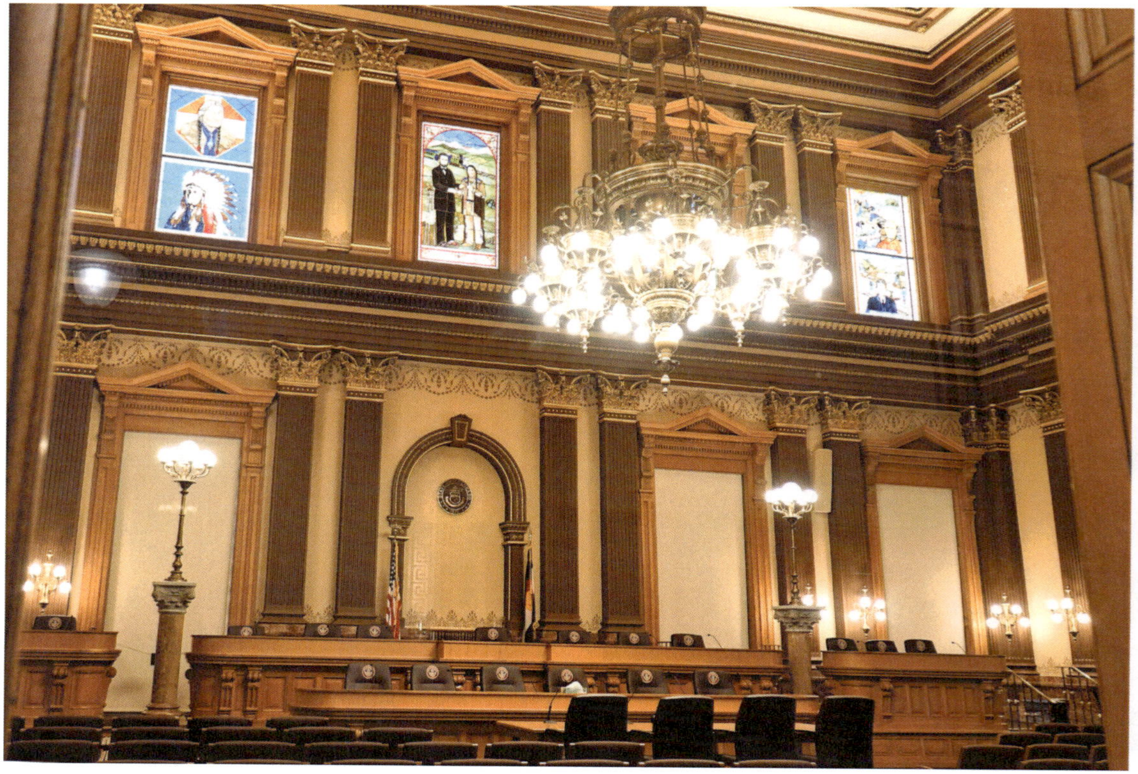

Stained-glass Artwork

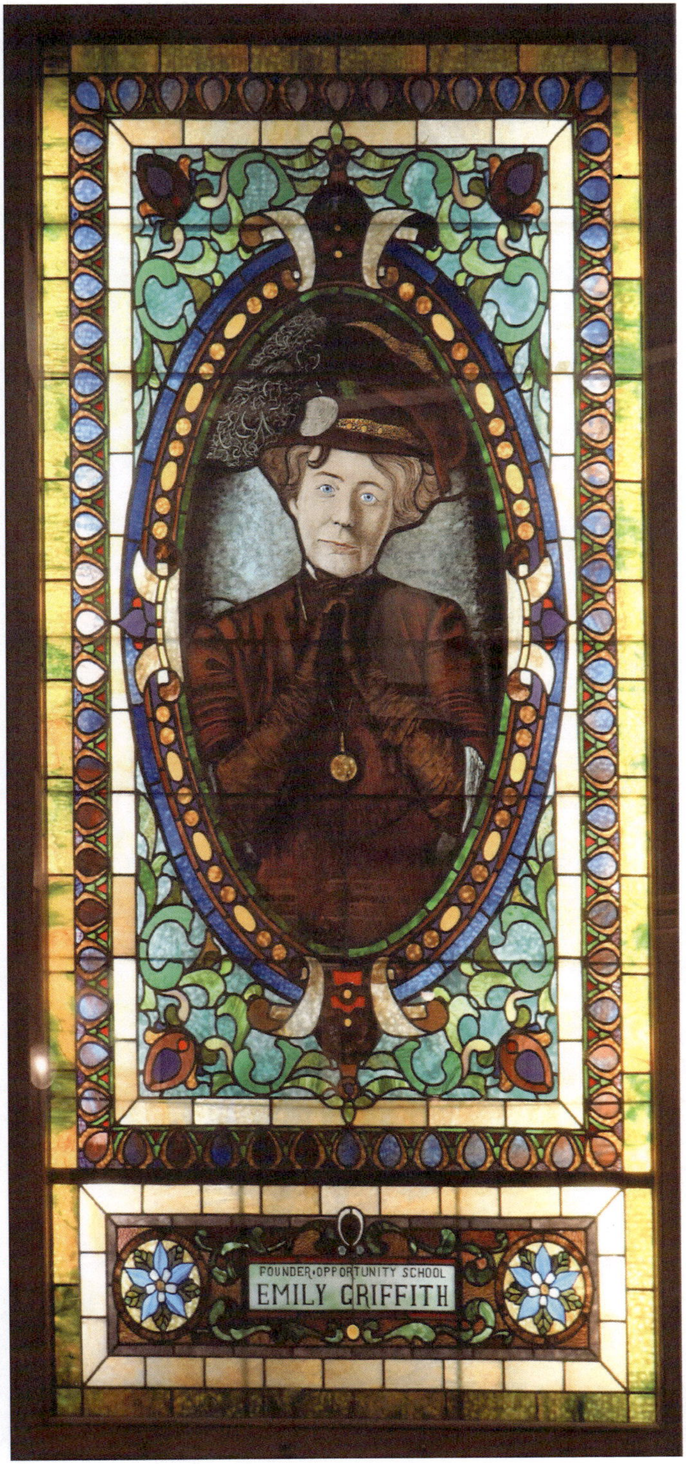

Many community and state leaders are honored with stained-glass depictions. One that holds a special location is Emily Griffith.

Emily Griffith was a teacher who believed education should be available to all people, no matter their age or financial situation.

She established the Opportunity School in 1916, offering free classes during the day and evening so students could attend when they were not working. She just wanted people to learn.

When a student fainted because of hunger, Emily started feeding both students' minds and their stomachs.
In 1933, the school's name was changed to Emily Griffith Opportunity School in her honor.

The stained-glass portrait was placed in the capitol in 1976 to honor her lasting impact on Colorado.

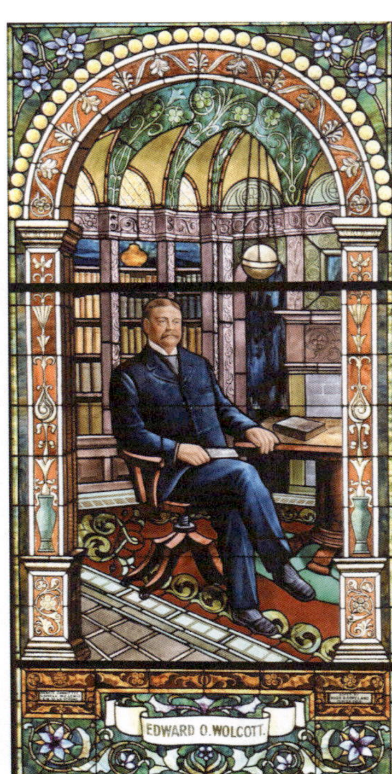

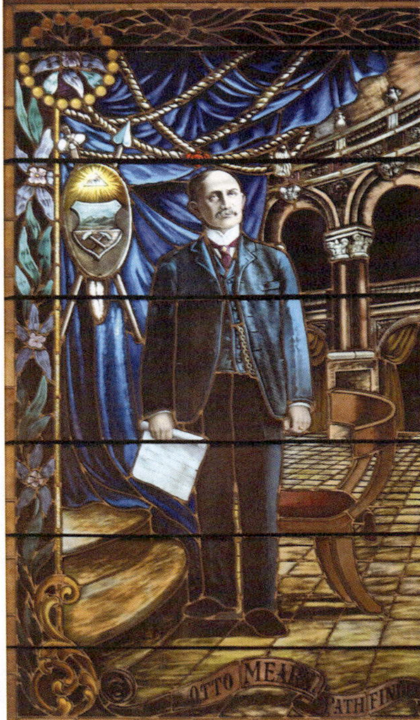

Murals Depicts Thomas Hornsby Ferril Poem

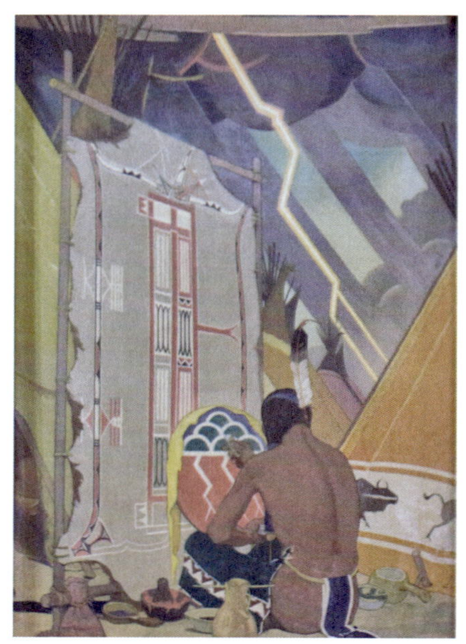

Men shall behold the Water in the Sky and count the Seasons by the living Grasses

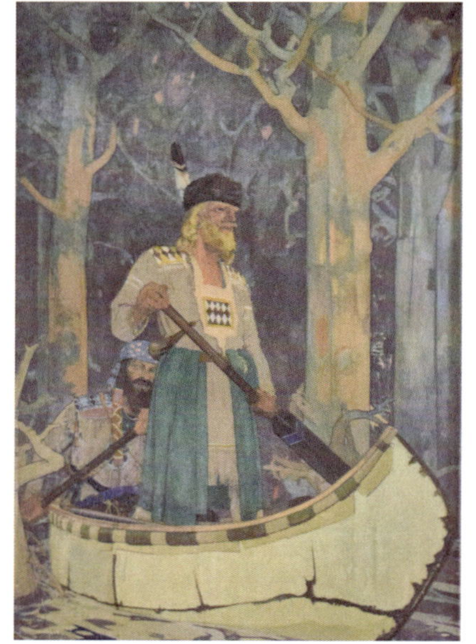

Then shall the River-namers track the Sunset Singing the long song to the Shining Mountain

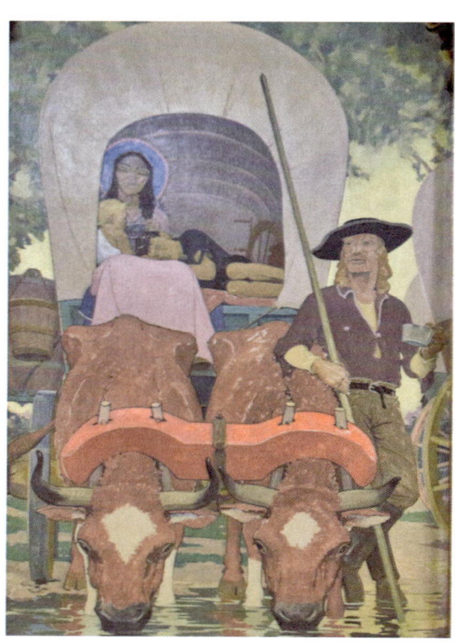

Here shall the melting Snows renew the Oxen here Firewood is and here shall Men

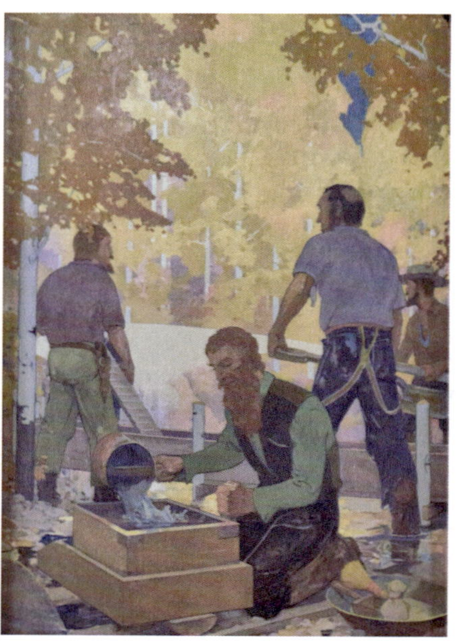

Water shall Sluice the Gold yellow as leaves that fall from Silver Trees on silent Hills

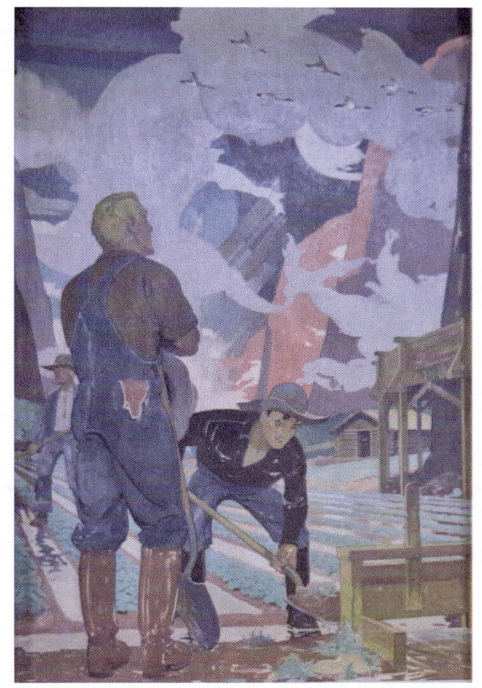

And Man shall
fashion
Glaciers into
Greenness
and harvest
April rivers in
the Autumn

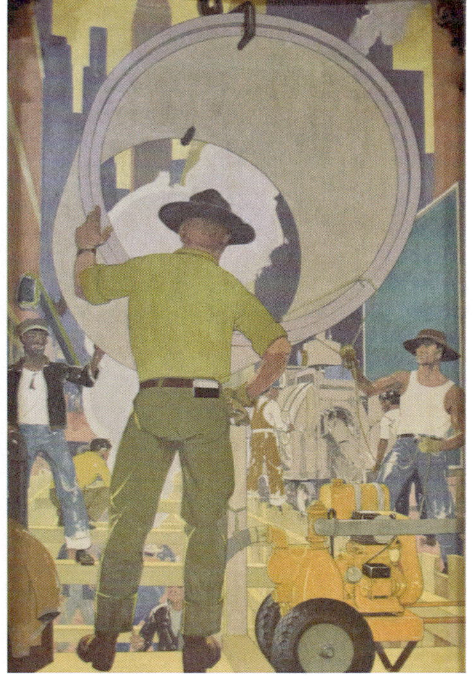

Deep in the
Earth where
roots of Willows
drank shall
Aqueducts be
laid to nourish
Cities

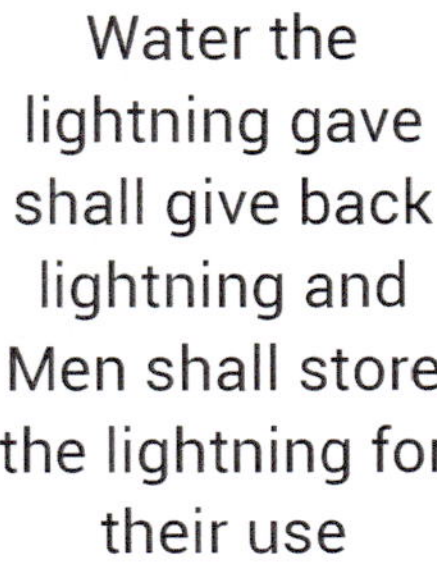

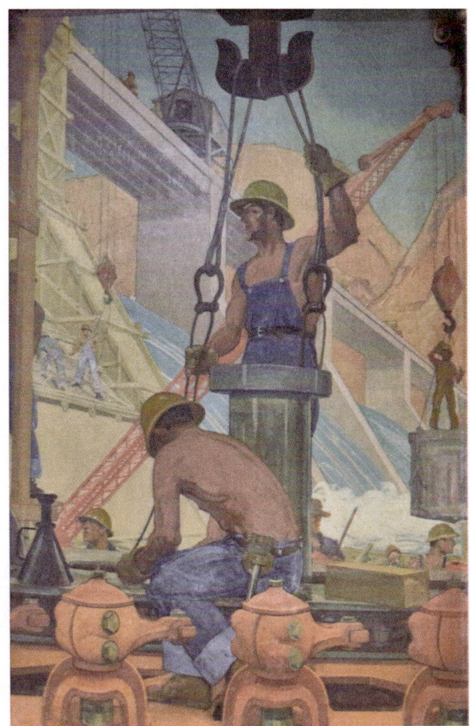

Water the
lightning gave
shall give back
lightning and
Men shall store
the lightning for
their use

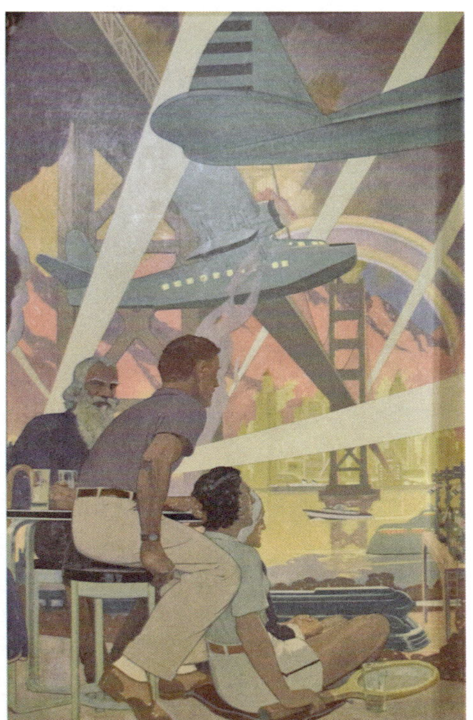

Beyond the
sundown is
Tomorrow's
Wisdom
today is going to
be long long ago

Brass Everywhere from Elevators to Doorknobs

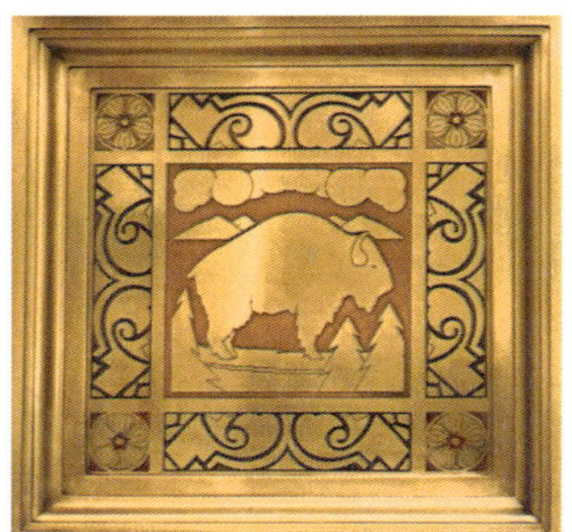

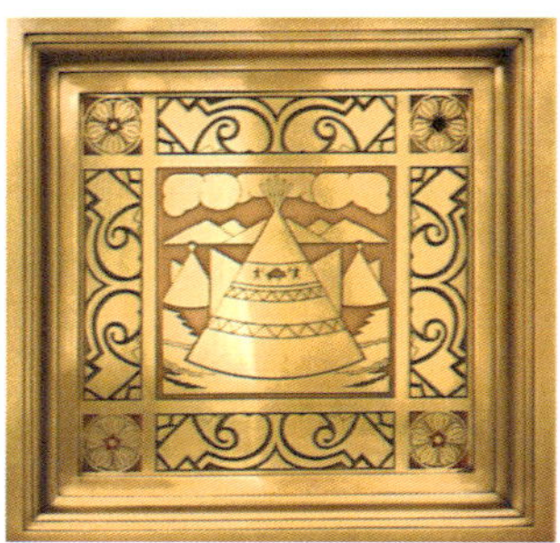

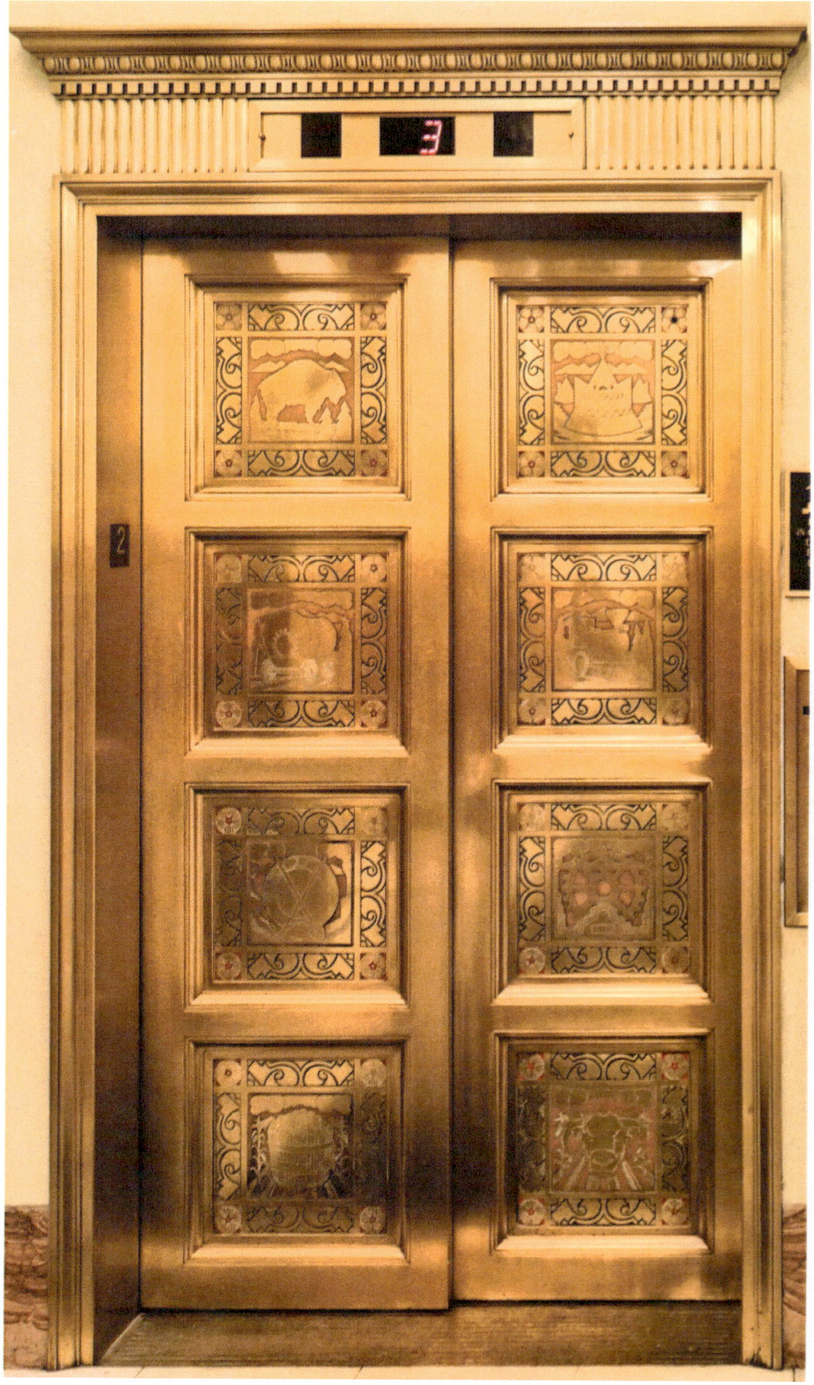

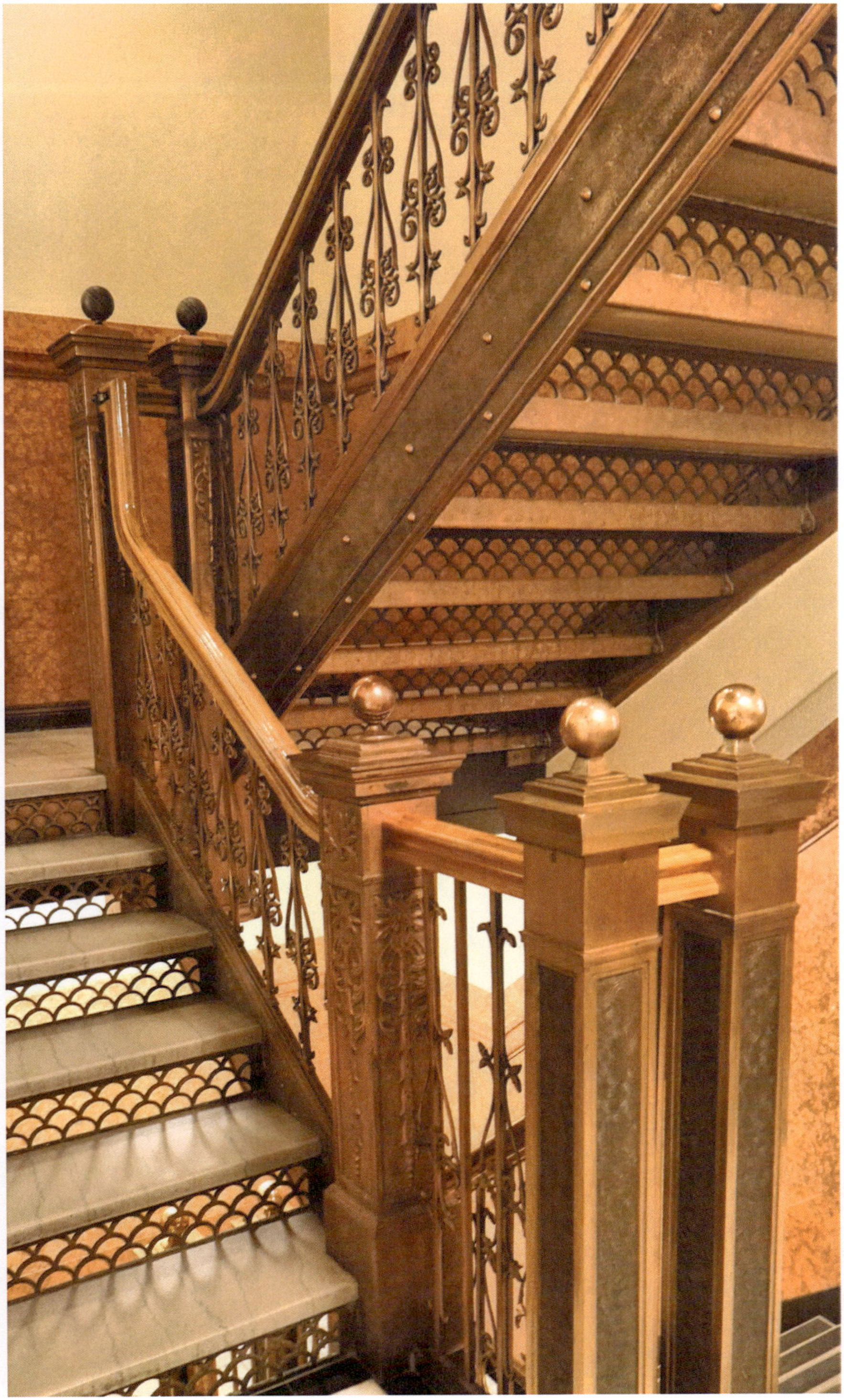

Secondary Stairway, Cannon Balls

Secondary stairway features decorative metal railing balustrades and cannon balls knobs on the newels.

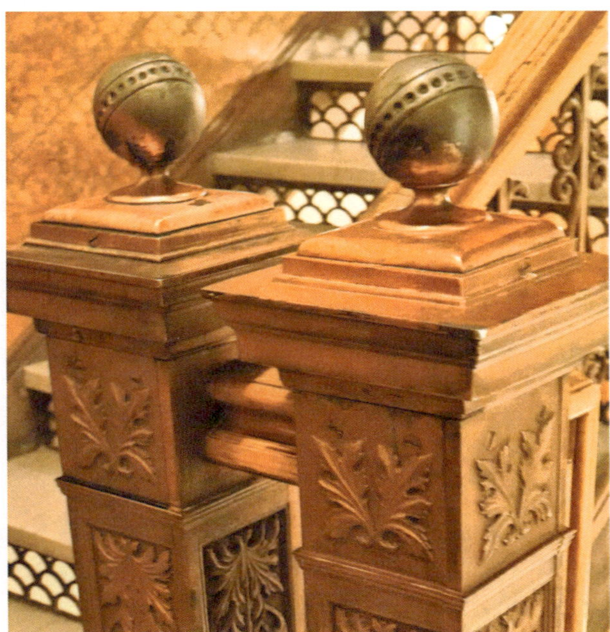

Colorado State Seal

Colorado's state seal was approved by the first General Assembly on March 15, 1877.

At the top is the eye of God within a triangle, from which golden rays radiate on two sides.

Below the eye is a scroll, the Roman fasces, a bundle of birch or elm rods with a battle axe bound together by red thongs and bearing on a band of red, white and blue, the words, "Union and Constitution."

The Roman fasces is the insignia of a republican form of government; the bundle of rods bound together symbolizes strength which is lacking in the single rod. The axe symbolizes authority and leadership.

Below the scroll is the heraldic shield bearing across the top three snow-capped mountains on a red background with clouds above them. The lower half of the shield has two miner's tools, the pick and sledgehammer, crossed on a golden ground.

Below the shield in a semi-circle is the motto "Nil Sine Numine," Latin for "nothing without the Deity." The year Colorado became a state, 1876, is printed at the bottom of the seal.

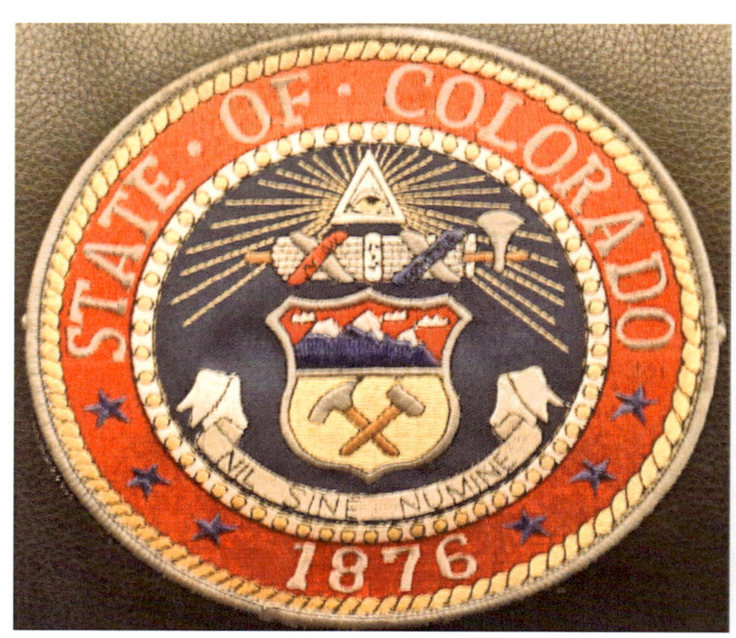

About the Photographer

Jane Moorman describes herself as an adventurer who loves to drive the backroads to see what there is to see.

During her 30-year journalism career, Jane honed her photographic skills as a photojournalist, including covering high school sporting events.

A friend once said, "I wish I could see the world as Jane sees it. Finding the beauty in things that most of us don't take time to see."

Upon retiring in 2021, Jane decided there is a lot of her native country she had not visited, including each state's capitol, so she began her journey of exploring the USA.

Jane currently lives in Albuquerque, New Mexico, but says her real home is on the road.

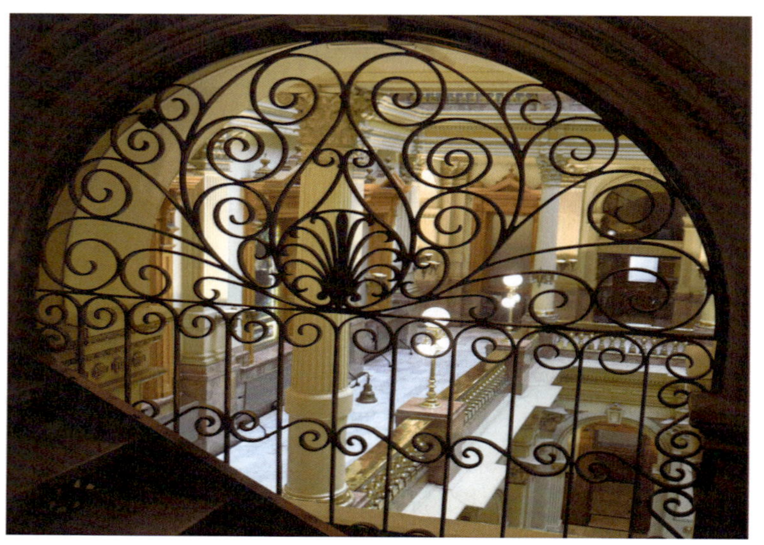

www.ingramcontent.com/pod-product-compliance
Lightning Source LLC
Chambersburg PA
CBRC092052150726
48005CB00031B/1010